Zadie Smith

# THE WIFE OF WILLESDEN

*Incorporating*:
The Wife of Willesden's Tale
*which tale is preceded by*
The General Lock-In
*and*
The Wife of Willesden's Prologue
*and followed by*
A Retraction

*Told in verse couplets*
*Translated from the Chaucerian into North Weezian*

*On the occasion of the Brent 2020*
*pilgrimage and celebration*

PENGUIN BOOKS

# THE WIFE OF WILLESDEN

By the same author

Presented by Kiln Theatre
in association with
Brent 2020, London Borough of Culture

PENGUIN BOOKS

UK | USA | Canada | Ireland | Australia
India | New Zealand | South Africa

Penguin Books is part of the Penguin Random House group of companies
whose addresses can be found at global.penguinrandomhouse.com.

First published 2021

002

Copyright © Zadie Smith, 2021

The publisher is grateful for permission to use, on p. 98, lyrics from 'Redemption Song',
written by Bob Marley © 1980 Fifty-Six Hope Road Music Ltd & Primary Wave/Blue Mountain
Music. Copyright renewed. All rights reserved. Used by permission.
All rights administered by Primary Wave/Blue Mountain Music.

The moral right of the author has been asserted

Text design by Richard Marston
Set in 12.5/16pt Fournier MT Std
Typeset by Jouve (UK), Milton Keynes
Printed and bound in Great Britain by Clays Ltd, Elcograf S.p.A.

The authorized representative in the EEA is Penguin Random House Ireland,
Morrison Chambers, 32 Nassau Street, Dublin DO2 YH68

A CIP catalogue record for this book is available
from the British Library

ISBN: 978-0-241-47196-8

www.greenpenguin.co.uk

Dedicated to the *Windrush* generation,
with much love and respect

# Contents

## Introduction
## From Chaucerian to North Weezian
## (via Twitter)

This is a weird one: sometime in early 2018, I got an email from one Lois Stonock, informing me that 'we' had won the bid to be London's Borough of Culture 2020. I'm ashamed to admit it took me a minute to work out who this 'we' was and how I was included in it. Then I remembered: a year earlier I'd agreed to add my name to Brent's bid although to be honest I had only the vaguest sense at the time of what I had said yes to, or what I would do if, out of the thirty-two boroughs of London, my beloved Brent somehow beat the statistical odds and won.

Brent won. Lois's emails picked up in their frequency. Would I write something about The Ends to celebrate The Ends? But this simple request proved difficult to manage. It was like being asked to breathe when breathing is sort of what you do on the regular. Everything I write is more or less about Brent, yet being explicitly *asked* to write about Brent sent me into a spiral of self-consciousness from which no writing seemed likely to emerge. Poor Lois kept emailing. The deadline crept closer. I worked myself up into a panic. Brent, I'd say to myself, as I sat at my desk, *Brent*. Brent! Brent? I tried getting more specific: Kilburn. The Kilburn High Road. So long, so wide and so old. During the writing of a novel of mine, *NW*, I'd read a lot about the Kilburn High Road and its history, and knew it was Celtic originally, then Roman, then Anglo-Saxon, with an ancient river buried deep beneath it. Once a part of Watling Street, it was a common route for medieval pilgrims, on their way to visit the shrine of St Albans, or the Black Madonna in St Mary's, Willesden. Some of those pilgrims no doubt took their rest at Kilburn Priory (est. 1134), a famed local nunnery of Augustinian canonesses. Yes, the especially pious pilgrims would have stopped there. But surely many more people – basic types like you and me – would have paused in one of the pubs, like the Red Lion (1444) or the Cock Tavern (1486) for some ale and a pie and a bit of chat . . .

One day, just as I received another anxious email from Lois, it happened that I spotted a copy of *The Canterbury Tales* on a shelf in front of me and, at a loss for what else to tell her, I spontaneously suggested that perhaps I could take this connection between Kilburn and Canterbury pilgrimages and translate the original Chaucer into the contemporary local vernacular: *The Brondesbury Tales*. Cute idea. But when I actually took down the Chaucer I was reminded that his tales are many and long and it might take me till 2030 to complete the task. Well, how about *The*

*Wife of Bath*? Alas, this, too, was long. Well, how about a few verses of it, like a short monologue, the text of which we could put in our excellent *Brent Magazine*, or maybe even have a local actress perform it at the Kiln Theatre? Such was the plan.*

About a month later, I was heading to Australia for a literary festival when Lois emailed me about approving a press release. But the attachment was taking too long to open on the bad airport Wi-Fi, so I said I was sure whatever it said was fine and I got on that plane. A day later I landed in Australia and opened my laptop to find dozens of emails – from friends, family, colleagues and some strangers – all eager to hear more about my 'first play'. Not having written a play – or ever considered writing one – I was understandably a bit perturbed. I phoned my agent, who also congratulated me on my first play, and suggested I take a look at Twitter, which was apparently full of still more people almost as surprised as I was to find I had written a play. I then tried blaming Lois, but indeed in her press release she had said nothing about a play, although perhaps the word 'monologue' was, in retrospect, easily misinterpreted. I sat for a while in Sydney Airport and looked deep

---

*Of course, nothing about 2020 went to plan. Brent 2020 – like so many other cultural events of that year – was radically transformed by Covid-19, and the play itself cancelled and delayed.

into the gaping void in myself where a play was meant to be. I went through my options: break own leg, contract short but serious illness, remain in Australia, explain to Twitter it was mistaken, or try to translate a fourteenth-century medieval text written in rhyming couplets into a contemporary piece about Kilburn . . .

Which is all to say, when I sat down to write *The Wife of Willesden* I had no idea it would end up being one of the more delightful writing experiences of my life. I think, when we talk about 'creativity', not enough is said about the interesting role that limits, rules and restrictions can play. In this case, the rules of the game were almost absurdly constricting: a medieval text – concerning sexual politics that would seem as distant as the moon – constructed in rhyming couplets from lines of ten syllables each. Yet from the moment Alyson opens her mouth –

> *Experience, though noon auctoritee*
> *Were in this world, were right ynogh to me*
> *To speke of wo that is in marriage*

– I knew that she was speaking to me, and that she was a Kilburn girl at heart. What started out as homework soon came to feel like a wonderful case of serendipity. For Alyson's voice – brash, honest, cheeky, salacious, outrageous, unapologetic – is one I've heard and loved all my life: in the flats, at school, in the playgrounds of my childhood and then the pubs of my maturity, at bus stops, in shops, and of course up and down the Kilburn High Road, any day of the week. The words may be different but the spirit is the same. I loved the task of finding new words to fit. But just because you're enjoying writing something doesn't mean – in my experience – that it's going well. Here Indhu Rubasingham, the formidable artistic director of the Kiln, was vital, both as first reader, dramaturgical advisor and final judge, for it would be up to Indhu to decide whether this play that she had neither asked for nor expected was a) actually a play and b) suitable for her theatre. So that became my new day job: turning Alyson from Bath into Alvita from Willesden, while trying to maintain Chaucer's beautiful colloquial flow, those ten-syllable lines that rhyme without heaviness, and sing without ever actually becoming music. Chaucer wrote of the people and for them, never doubting that even the most rarefied religious, political and philosophical ideas could be conveyed in the language the people themselves speak. I have tried to maintain that democratic principle here.

When the play was finished, and Indhu decided to stage it in full – and for more than the single night I'd imagined – I don't think I have ever been more astounded in my life, nor more thrilled. To me, the Kiln is a sacred space: as a child I took drama lessons there, back when it was still the Tricycle, and I remember mourning the disastrous fire, and sharing in the local delight when a new theatre rose out of the ashes. I had so many of my earliest seminal theatrical experiences here. The Kiln is where I saw *The Colour of Justice*, about the Stephen Lawrence inquiry. It's where I first saw *Playboy of the West Indies*. The only way I could make sense of adding myself to the history of this storied stage was by remembering that it's really Chaucer up there – I'm only hiding in the folds of his garment.

It must seem, to many, an odd partnership. When I started writing, it often felt that way to me, too. The distance between Canterbury and Kilburn, and between the fourteenth century and the twenty-first, looked epic. But I wasn't very long on the road before the sympathetic rhymes between the two became audible and then deafening. '*Sovereigntee*' began to sound a lot like 'consent', for example, and Alyson's insistence on physical pleasure not unlike the sex-positivity movement, while her contempt for class privilege feels uncannily close to our debates on that topic today. Even the act of sexual violence that sits shockingly at the centre of her tale – and the restorative justice Alyson offers as a possible example of progressive punishment – read, to me, as absolutely contemporary. But that all makes it sound as if Alyson is a dogmatic sort, keen to impart serious moral and social lessons to her audience. Nothing could be further from the truth. Alyson shares with my own Alvita (I hope!) a startling indifference to the opinions of others and a passionate compulsion to live her own life as she pleases.

She has nothing to hide. Her desire to dominate men she freely admits; her own occasional hypocrisies she does not disguise; her insatiable appetite for life she announces to all. Personally, I could listen to her day and night, but having been to the theatre myself, and being aware that audiences generally prefer plays to involve more than one person, I made the decision early on to parcel out some of Alyson's scattershot wisdom and opinions to the various other people she speaks about, for and through.

Still, despite the fact that Alyson has turned into Alvita – and then been split many times over into all her husbands and friends – the text is, for the most part, a direct transposition of the Wife of Bath's prologue and tale. Here and there I have made judgement calls, substituting contemporary references for ones I thought too obscure to be meaningful to contemporary audiences. For example, the Pardoner, the Summoner and the Friar – all of whom make brief appearances in the Wife of Bath's prologue – have been transformed, respectively, into their modern vocational equivalents: a charity chugger, a bailiff, and the minister of a local megachurch. I have also taken a few liberties with the structure. All of Chaucer's tales are framed and bookended by the opening General Prologue and the final Retraction; the same is true here, but I have radically paraphrased – and mercifully shortened – both. The greatest change, perhaps, is in the tale itself, which has been switched from Arthurian England to eighteenth-century Jamaica. Try as I might, I couldn't imagine Alvita using King Arthur as a point of reference. These transformations aside, I'm proud to call the Wife of Bath and the Wife of Willesden half-sisters. I've so enjoyed my time with both of these wild women. I'd like to claim Alvita is the more feisty of the two, but the truth is you'll find all her feistiness in the original. That said, she certainly is more Kilburn and more Jamaica. She nah easy and she talk her mind.

# *Dramatis Personae*

In order of appearance

ALVITA, THE WIFE OF WILLESDEN  *A Jamaican-born British woman in her mid-fifties*

AUTHOR  *A brown woman in a headwráp*

PUBLICAN  POLLY  *The woman who runs the Colin Campbell pub*

AUNTIE P  *Alvita's churchgoing aunt*

PASTOR JEGEDE  *A Nigerian minister at a North London megachurch*

KELLY  *Alvita's very shy niece*

HUSBAND NO. 1, IAN  *An older, white Englishman*

HUSBAND NO. 2, DARREN  *A young, good-looking bwoy*

HUSBAND NO. 3, WINSTON  *A Rastaman*

HUSBAND NO. 4, ELRIDGE  *A well-to-do gentleman in his fifties, of Caribbean heritage*

HUSBAND NO. 5, RYAN  *A Scottish student doing his Masters*

GOD

ST PAUL

BLACK JESUS

*Dramatis Personae*

ZAIRE  *Alvita's best friend*
COLIN  *A charity chugger in his early twenties*
SOPHIE  *Colin's fiancée*
NELSON MANDELA
ASMA  *Local rebel wife*
SOCRATES
ERIPHYLE  *A bad wife of legend*
ARRIUS  *A vengeful husband of legend*
BARTOSZ  *A local bailiff*
STAGEHAND 1  *A child*
STAGEHAND 2  *A child*
QUEEN NANNY  *Our Maroon hero of Old Jamaica*
YOUNG MAROON  *A soldier in Queen Nanny's army*
OLD WIFE  *An Obeah woman of advanced years*

The same actors play:
*Author, Kelly, Zaire, Eriphyle and Queen Nanny*
*Publican Polly, God and Sophie*
*Auntie P and Old Wife*
*Pastor Jegede and Husband Elridge*
*Husband Ian, St Paul, Socrates, Arrius and Bartosz*
*Husband Darren, Colin and Young Maroon*
*Husband Winston, Black Jesus and Nelson Mandela*

Incidental characters and choruses are
played by members of the cast.

*The Wife of Willesden*

# THE GENERAL LOCK-IN

We are inside the Colin Campbell, a small pub on the Kilburn High Road. The sun is setting on the celebrations of the announcement: Brent is to be the Borough of Culture for 2020. People are pouring into the pub for refreshment and rest. A large banner above the bar reads: 'The Kilburn High Road Pub Crawl'. Another sign reads: 'BRENT BOROUGH OF CULTURE: 2020'.

The Campbell is a quiet pub, usually occupied by a few all-day lone drinkers, but today these old men in their wrinkled suits are suddenly inundated by a colourful crowd. There's been dancing; some people are in carnival-like costume; there are people in their national dress, families, teenagers, lovers. Every possible kind of person. The bar staff struggle to serve the influx of people and seat them all, but after a bit of kerfuffle, most have a table, and now begin opening packets of crisps, or their own tubs of home-made food . . .

There is, in one corner, a little makeshift stage, with a home-made sign hanging behind: 'Celebrating Local Stories'. A red-headed young man with his back to the audience has *a video camera on a stand, ready to film whoever comes up to talk — but people seem reluctant. Music is playing, footie is on the TV, we can't hear the people, but we see lots of little local dramas and conversations playing out, and may notice one especially striking woman,* ALVITA, WIFE OF WILLESDEN. *She's settling seating arguments, she's handing over pints to people who can't reach the bar, laughing and joking with everyone . . .*

*In one corner, the* AUTHOR *sits, quieter than the rest, with a laptop on her table.*

AUTHOR
It was the summer of 2019.
I was back home, checking the local scene
And the whole neighbourhood was in the streets
To celebrate the recent local feat:
Winning the London Borough of Culture.
Call it a pilgrimage: all together
We crawled down Kilburn High Road, until we
Reached the Colin Campbell. We drank. Polly
Bailey, who runs it, suggested a

WHOLE CAST
*LOCK-IN!*

PUBLICAN POLLY
Let's get our drink on with the whole block.
And, wait, listen: here's what we're gonna do:
From right now till . . . let's say . . . half past two
We'll have a little contest. Your stories
On that stage. I'll be the judge and MC.
And when everyone's told their tale, the best
One will receive a full English Breakfast
Tomorrow morning, on the house. *With* chips.

*All cheer.*

AUTHOR
Everyone got on their open-mic tip . . .
We had all types of people in that night,
Young and old, rich and poor, black, brown and white –
But local: students, merchants, a bailiff,
People from church, temple, mosque, shul. And if
There's a person in Brent who doesn't think
Their own life story isn't just the thing
To turn into a four-hundred-page book
I'd like to meet them. So off they went. Look
At them.

*We see people encouraging each other up to tell short stories*
*from their life, and the reaction of the crowds.*

       All telling their stories. Mostly
Men. Not because they had better stories
But because they had no doubt that we should
Hear them. The night wore on. I wondered: Would
A woman speak? And one or two did. But
Like the men – like most of us – they said what
They thought others wanted to hear. Or lied,
Or humble-bragged, or said the nice, polite
Clichéd things that nice people like to say . . .

*We see a man and woman on the stage together and we hear*
*the following snippet.*

FEMALE SPEAKER
He's just 'the one' – we get married in May.
He's like my rock? Wouldn't you say so, Steven?

MALE SPEAKER
Yeah: everything happens for a reason
And we're just meant to be! Our stars aligned.

FEMALE SPEAKER
It's Fate! (Our gift registry's online.)

AUTHOR
Some said 'brave' things that took no bravery
To say, or were dull, or didn't move me –
Or spoke about their 'journeys' with an air
Of triumph. I was starting to despair . . .
Then I saw Alvita. That is: the Wife
Of Willesden. And the story of her life's
Worth hearing.

RYAN
Tho' she's a bit deaf herself
In one ear . . . but otherwise in good health.

WINSTON
And skilful! Makes her own clothes, every stitch.
That's not Armani – that's Alvita!

ASMA
                       Rich
She is not. But she never passed a *Big
Issue* vendor without chucking a quid
Their way.

WINSTON
Cuss you if *you* don't.

ZAIRE

        Fake gold chains
Are her jewellery of choice. She drips like rain.

DARREN

Her underwear is dramatic – and red.
Like the soles of her knock-off 'Choos'. It's said
She looks bold. She gives side-eye perfectly.

ZAIRE

   She's been *that bitch* since 1963.

RYAN

And yeah, she's been hitched five times to five men.

WINSTON

(Without counting back-in-the-day bredrin.)

ASMA

But we don't need to get into that now.
She's a well-travelled woman. She allows
Herself adventures. Self-care is her truth.
She's been Ibiza, Corfu, Magaluf.

DARREN
She likes to wander. Hates to be tied down.
With that gap-toothed smile she strides around town
Dressed to impress.

ZAIRE
     Wears an *isicholo*:
A big Zulu hat. She's not Zulu, no . . .
But let woman have her hat!

WINSTON
             And a skirt
That shows her shape.

DARREN
And them shoes that will hurt
You if you're in her way.

ASMA
     She's not just fierce
Though. She's sweet and wise. Cupid's dart has pierced
Her so often, she's an expert on love.

DARREN
Been there, done that. This one knows it all, bruv.

*We see* ALVITA *being ushered towards the little stage, but she refuses it, and instead takes her rightful place, centre stage in the Colin Campbell. The pub turns black: there is a theatrical spotlight upon her. But before she speaks, the scene freezes while the* AUTHOR *gives her Chaucerian apologia . . .*

AUTHOR
But before she starts, a word to the wise:
Not a trigger warning, exactly, but
A proviso: it's not my tale. I just
Copied it down from the original.
I could make stuff up and rewrite it all
But that would surely defeat the purpose,
And if Alvita does make you nervous
It's worth remembering – though I'm sure you know –
When wives spoke thus six hundred years ago
You were all shocked *then*. The shock never ends
When women say things usually said by men . . .
And one last thing: if you spot yourself and
Think I've made you posher or more common
Than you'd like: sorry. I've got a good ear,
But I can only write down what I hear . . .

THE WIFE OF WILLESDEN'S PROLOGUE

ALVITA *reanimates and the* AUTHOR *withdraws to her table. Throughout the Prologue,* ALVITA *regularly breaks the fourth wall, speaking to the real audience as much as the pub one. Her accent is North Weezy with moments of deliberate poshness as well as frequent lapses into Jamaican patois and cockney for comic effect. She is a world-class raconteur. She begins:*

ALVITA
Let me tell you something: I do not need
Any permission or college degrees
To speak on how marriage is *stress*. I been
Married five damn times since I was nineteen!
From mi eye deh a mi knee.* But I survived,
Thank God, and I got to say, of the five,
None of them were total wastemen. But last
Week . . .

---

*Patois: 'From back when my eyes were at my knees.' That is, 'Since I was a small child.'

15

*At this point the lights come up again, but there is something surreal about the new lighting in the pub, as if we are in a magical, liminal space between storytelling, memory and reality. The pub people react and laugh and groan like an audience, but they are often roped into the performance, too. Some of these moments are explicitly noted below, but a director should feel free to use the* PUB CHORUS *to animate and dramatize as many of Alvita's stories as they see fit.*

I'm with my Auntie P, yeah, and she starts
In on her Bible talk:

AUNTIE P
                              Yuh nuh know Christ
Him a wedding guest one time in him life?
In Cana, Galilee? Please, niece, beg yuh
Tell me what you do the opposite for?
How come you believe you can get wedded
Five times? Lawd knows how many times bedded!
Tink when Jesus met the Samaritan,
By dat well: 'member how he cuss her, man,
Him seh, 'Woman, you been married five times
Already. You can't say *this man ah fi mi*
Because nutten nuh go so. Not at all.

ALVITA
And I was like, look, Auntie, you can bawl
Me out, but I still don't even get why
He said that? She married the first five guys.
So why not six? Is there a set limit?
With me, I'm almost fifty-five, innit,
And if there *is* a right number of men,
That's news to me. Is it six or eight? Ten?
In my view, people got too much to say;
They chat rubbish. But from my Bible days
I know it says:

*We hear church music and see church lighting, and we meet*
PASTOR JEGEDE *in the middle of a sermon.* AUNTIE P
*and* KELLY *are listening intently.*

PASTOR JEGEDE
                'Go forth and multiply.'

ALVITA
I remember the bits that weren't too dry . . .
And isn't it that God said when they married:

PASTOR JEGEDE
A husband must leave his old family,
And link up mind, body and soul—

17

ALVITA

With me! Yep. Nothing about bigamy
In there, or more-gamy-than-that (cough, cough).
So how come some people slagging me off?
Nah, I'm not having it. Count the pickney
And women of Marley. How 'bout Stevie?
Now, you know Stevie's had more than one wife!
Blindness don't stop him enjoying his life.
I should be so lucky as Bob Marley.
Rita? Miss Jamaica? He had plenty
Woman, and I'm sure he had a good time
With them all, back in the day. And that's fine.
But let's also thank God for *my* five men:
Ian, Darren, Winston, Elridge and Ryan.

*As this is said we see Alvita's husbands*, IAN, DARREN,
WINSTON, ELRIDGE *and* RYAN – *who are dotted around
the pub – stand up and start looking at each other curiously.
We may not notice that the fifth husband*, RYAN, *is the red-
head with the video camera, who we can't really see: the video
equipment obscures his face. When he stands it must look as if
he is just doing something to his camera. After a moment they
sit back down again.*

(You think five's a lot? I could've had ten!)
But I'm well choosy. I actually picked them
For their *ass*-ets, different for each person.
One went to the College of North West London,
Two went to the School of Hard Knocks. The sick
Thing about Kilburn is how we can mix
It up with anyone? High, low. Posh, poor.
We've had practice. We'll walk through any door.
And that's like me spending my time studying
Five different husbands. You learn many things . . .
And, honestly, I'm up for Number Six
Whenever, wherever he feels to pitch
Up. Serious: if Five drops dead, boom, like that:
I won't wait for my hymen to grow back.
That's not me. You'll soon see me on Insta
Chucking the bouquet to the next sista . . .
Pastor, if your man dies, you're free, innit?
To get hitched again, if you feel like it.

PASTOR JEGEDE *looks like he doesn't want to concede this*
*point; also these questions are disturbing his service, which, in*
*a parallel reality, is happening throughout.*

Auntie P, isn't St Paul the one who said

AUNTIE P
Better to be married than burn up dead!

ALVITA
But in your church, the one on Willesden Lane

*We hear church music again, and see* AUNTIE P *and her*
SONS *praying in the pub, with* PASTOR JEGEDE *leading*
*the prayers.*

The old Bingo place, you go fill your brain
With judgement. Pastor chatting all that breeze:

PASTOR JEGEDE
. . . Wicked Lamech, whose sin was bigamy . . .

ALVITA
How come Jacob and Abraham marry
Again? And I'm sure Pastor put a ring
On it a few times in Nigeria . . .

AUNTIE P
All I know is that the Lord God him nuh
Like looseness. Him defend de marriage bond.

ALVITA
Yeah, but Auntie, the thing is, that's just wrong?
Where do you think you read that? The Good Book?
You can't show it to me. S'not there. I've looked.

AUNTIE P
Me know him defended virginity.

ALVITA
Now hol' up, hol' up, my dear Auntie P:
Thing is: I can read just like you can read,
And I'm telling you no. It's true Paul said
He didn't want us having sex for fun –
But it weren't like: COMMANDMENT NUMBER ONE.
Auntie, what you call laws I call advice!
A guideline. And they all sound very nice,
But everyone got to make their own choice
In life. And if God in his big God voice
Was like:

GOD
            Everyone. Asexual. NOW.

ALVITA
It wouldn't make no sense. Because then how's
He expecting to make more pure virgins

When there's nobody to give birth to them?
*Please*. At least St Paul wasn't all about
Cancelling things God himself hadn't called out!

PASTOR JEGEDE
We aim for chastity. This is the prize.
The contest is to be pure in God's eyes.

KELLY, *Alvita's very nerdy, shy and put-upon niece, dares to raise her voice:*

KELLY
But that's not, like, meant for . . . well, like, maybe –

ALVITA
Yes, girl – g'wan – *Say* it! (That's my niece, Kelly.)

KELLY
Maybe that's not meant for everybody?
Like, Mum, maybe God makes some people true
Saints, yeah? But with some he's like: s'up to you . . .
Like, I totally get Jesus was pure
And he was into that but are you sure
It's got to be like that for me and you?

ALVITA

This is what I'm saying! Kelly, *thank* you.
Bottom line, Auntie, I have permission
From bloody St Paul himself to go fishing
For husbands when and where I feel like it.
The only thing I'm willing to admit
Is you probably have to wait till one dies
Before you move on, because bigamy-wise
That'd be an issue.

PASTOR JEGEDE

                    It is clearly
Said, by the apostle, that purity
Is best.

ALVITA

Yeah, but he was chatting about
Himself! St Paul be like:

ST PAUL/HUSBAND IAN

   I won't go out
With you. I will not come back to your place.
I won't submit to your sinful embrace.
We're not 'getting it on' on your sofa.

ALVITA
A holy man plus a supernova
Like me? You put us together? There will
Be fireworks, you get me? There just will.
But their church says:

AUNTIE P
                              Best to sleep with no one!

ALVITA
Wait – check it:

PASTOR JEGEDE
                    But if you marry someone –
And this is true for our women and our men –
It is best never to have sex with them.

ALVITA
Jokers. Fools. But it don't even touch me.
I don't mess with churchmen *or* my family.
My thing is: you want to think you're a saint?
Fine. But don't slut-shame me because I ain't
About that. It's not like I'm pretending
To be picture perfect. Or curating
My life for others. Despite what you see
Online, we're not all on yachts in Bali.

Some of us are on the ninety-eight bus
Which comes on time, and that's enough for us . . .
Auntie, I think God loves variety,
That's my belief. Cos if he *did* make me
He set my soul on its own strange path. Plus
Maybe he gives out sex like Santa Claus:
The nice get no sex drives; the nasty . . . more.
Maybe it just depends. Maybe if you're
Asexual or abstain he's into that . . .
That'd make sense cos his son was like that –
But you make everything so literal!
You really reckon Jesus meant to tell
Us all to be as broke as him? Nah. He's
Just saying:

BLACK JESUS
            You can be brassic like me
If you think you can handle it, but 'low
It for everybody else.

ALVITA
            For real, now,
Them rules are for the girl who feels that she's
Perfect. And that blatantly isn't me.
As you see, I'm in the prime of my life
And right now I'm into being a wife.

*My* kind of wife. Cos, tell me, Auntie P.
This equipment between our legs which we
Carry: why d'we have them in the first place?
Or you reckon it's some kind of mistake?

AUNTIE P
Wat a way yuh like fi argue me down!
But I believe our . . . private parts . . . they around
Fi two purpose. Fi pass the urine. And
Know who ah woman and who ah man.

ALVITA
Auntie's a comedian. But she knows
Well from experience how these things go.
It's crazy to me that Pastor gets mad
When I talk about women's pleasure and
The idea that if there *is* a God he
Can't hate on his own gift, which he must see
Is not just for making babies or . . . wee.
Pastor, it's right there in the book! Let's read
It:

PASTOR JEGEDE
'Man owes a debt to his wife.'

ALVITA
In bed!
That is literally what the man said!
And to pay that sexual debt in full,
You usually need your own genitals.
Look: my point is, we're given these things
For more than childbirth and urinating!

ZAIRE, *Alvita's best friend, raises her hand.*

ZAIRE
But just cos you have working genitals
We don't *have* to go down the kid road? All
Of us don't need babies. It's cool if your
Road is kids. But that's not all these are for.

ALVITA
(My bestie, Zaire.) And then there's Jesus:
So pure and holy he's just not that fussed
Re sex. And I've got nothing against pure,
Holier-than-thou people. I think you're
All great. But there's a lot of different kinds
Of women in this world. Some like red wine
Thirty quid a pop. You know who you are!
I'll take a shot of Baileys at the bar.
I'm that kind of girl. Not fancy but fun,

27

Like Baileys. Sweet. And I get the job done.
My thing is, to be honest, I'm just real.
I do and say exactly what I feel.
I'm not fussy, but I stick to my guns
And in *my* marriage I'll use *this* for fun.
If it's God's gift, I best use it that way!
Cos if I waste it, what's God gonna say?
Now, husbands: I was and am here for you:
Tonight, tomorrow. But you need to do
Something for me first. I demand pleasure.
That is your debt to me. It's not pressure,
Exactly, it's about consent. You'll agree
To owe me love, good sex, and that when we
Marry, your body and soul will be mine
As long as we're a thing. From that time
Till we're done, your body is my playground,
It's for me, not for you. I've just found
That really works for me? In fact, St Paul's
The one gave me the idea. Cos he's all
About

ST PAUL
'You husbands! Love your women well, day in
Day out!'

ALVITA
Thank you! That's all I've been saying!

*There is applause from the tables, but some consternation, too, especially from some of the men.*

Any questions? Comments? So far, so clear?
Yes, you: don't be shy. Loud – so I can hear.

COLIN, *a nervous young man in a charity chugger outfit, stands up. His fiancée,* SOPHIE, *sits beside him.*

COLIN
Hello . . . well, my name's Colin . . . I work for—

ALVITA
You hassle fools in the street for cash – sure –

COLIN
Well, actually I raise money to fight—

ALVITA
You get their sort codes. Make them feel all right
About themselves. Mug them for a good cause.
But tell me: how can I help you and yours?

COLIN

Um . . . well, this is Soph, we just got engaged . . .
And a lot of what you said tonight made
Me feel a bit anxious, if I'm honest.

ALVITA

Is it. Go on . . . I don't bite, I promise.

COLIN

Like, are you saying that if I marry
She owns me? I find that a bit scary –
Like, in my view, that's taking things a bit
Too far, like: sexism – but reversing it?

ALVITA

I see, Colin. Thing is, though, my story's
Not even started yet? So don't worry:
Try not to wag the tail before the dog.
This bit's just the – whadyacallit – *Prologue*.
I'm about to drop knowledge on you,
Colin, and on your lovely girlfriend, too.
Because I've been there, Colin; this ain't my
First rodeo. And I'm using my *time*,
My *precious* time, to help needy men
Like you, not to make total fools of them

Selves in marriage. That is my mission.
Best thing you can do? Sit up and listen.

COLIN
Yes, ma'am – I mean, Miss – I mean, Mrs – Miz?
Of course, I know you know your business,
Wife of Willesden – I shouldn't interrupt.
You know what? I'll own my privilege – and shut up.

ALVITA
Young men: if you think you can stand to hear
Some truth I'll tell it. But if you start to fear
I'm running my mouth, talking wild and rough,
Or I've said too much, please don't take the huff –
Or get offended; don't be *that* guy . . .
I might take the piss – but I'll tell no lies.
So let's get down to it: those men I've had?
Three of them were good and two were bad.

*We see the* FIVE MEN *identified as she mentions them, but
again, that* RYAN *is one of them remains unclear.*

ALVITA
The three good ones were – bad news for Colin –
Older. They'd already found their place in

31

This world. But they had their work cut out
In the bedroom, because I'm all about
Pleasure, and they couldn't always keep
Up with my desire. They needed their sleep.
To be honest, it didn't bother me.
They made up for it in maturity.
With these young'uns you need a magic potion
To get their love, respect and devotion.
Back when I was young I worked way too hard
For approval; I'd put all my damn cards
On the table. Now I have no need. Since
I hold them in my hand. I can rinse
Out their bank accounts, move into their
Flats – they'd give me all, if I asked. But where
And when and why should I be asking
For love? The sun is out: I am basking
In affection. Meanwhile they have work
To do up in the bedroom. Learn to twerk,
For example: that's a useful skill in

*Here we might see a number of older men in the* PUB CHORUS
*trying to master this task.*

A man. That's something really worth learning!
But the older dogs are less
Inclined to learn; they want to get their rest.

Fine. But I still ruled them with a firm hand.
I cussed them daily, and they'd understand,
And be grateful, *so* relieved, when I turned
Nice. And that's one key thing I have learned
About marriage. You've got to treat them mean
To keep them loving and humble and keen.
Let me break it down: when a husband
Shows his cards; you've got to hide your hand.
Before he gets on your case, get on his.
I'd be like: first thing, handle your business.
What were you doing at that girl's place?
Are you really going to say to my face:

HUSBAND DARREN
I went to check my cousin – he's crashing there.
Didn't really notice . . . what's her name? Claire?

ALVITA
Bruv, I've seen her: fake nails, fake boobs, fake hair –
You're gonna do me like that? Is that fair?
And then meanwhile, if I'm just jamming
With a male friend, you're sure we're banging,
You lose your mind, cuss me up and down . . .
Double standard! But that's what I've found
About husbands. They chat too much breeze
About women. Got way too many theories.

33

I've heard them all.

HUSBAND WINSTON
                    Don't trust a gold digger;
They've got plans for you. Dem fine figures
Are a trap, yuh know? Dey ah go reel you in.
You'll pay in cash; it's the wages of sin.
Not love they want, man, it's alimony.

ALVITA
And then there's:

HUSBAND IAN
                    Avoid the ones with money:
They'll emasculate you. When a man
Earns less than his wife you'll find he can't
Respect himself. That's not just my view,
That's in evolutionary science, too.

ALVITA
Yeah, yeah, yeah. And if she's very pretty
God help her.

HUSBAND DARREN
                    Must be doing you dirty,
Because no one that fit could be faithful—

ALVITA
According to you. For some men it's awful
If a woman is rich or hot or fine
Or smart or talented or sweet or kind –
Cos that means someone else might want us.
And everything you once loved about us
Becomes the problem. If we still attract
Attention, then:

HUSBAND ELRIDGE
                                You ask for it. The fact
Is, it's your fault.

ALVITA
                        If we no longer do,
That's worse. We might go grind on a fool
'Pon the dance floor just for attention.

*The pub becomes a nightclub and we see* ALVITA *joyfully
dancing with a number of her* HUSBANDS *and others.*

And then slyly, casually, he mentions
That he can't remember why he chose
*This*. He could be playing Tinder. Who knows
How sweet life could be if he were free?
But deep down? It's all insecurity.

Some husbands are wound up way too tight.
Some of dem on that jealousy tip night
And day:

HUSBAND ELRIDGE
          The thing about women is they
Act a certain way up until the day
You wed. Then it's a whole other story.
New becomes old. Fresh becomes boring.
The pink cammy gets switched for grey cotton . . .
All that tear-your-clothes-off sex? Forgotten.

ALVITA
And so on. He'll say:

HUSBAND ELRIDGE
                    When a man buys clothes
He gets to try stuff on before he goes
And buys it. With wives? You roll the dice and see!

ALVITA
Honestly, sometimes this man made me
Want to scream. And he'd try to turn it round.
He'd say:

HUSBAND ELRIDGE
            The truth is you love the sound
Of men singing your praises. You call
Yourself a feminist but you want all
The compliments all the time. If you say
*How does this look?* am I free to lay
It on the line? Come on now. We both
Know my duties. I've got to swear on oath
You look like Angela Bassett. *All*
The time. For your birthday you want a ball.
You want me to hire out Camden Palais
And pay for it all. Then you want me to say
I love all your girlfriends, even that one
Claims she's a 'life coach' but lives with her mum.


*There has been much laughter in the pub and music and re-*
*enactment during* ELRIDGE'*s speech but now the lighting*
*becomes stark and everything is silent as* ALVITA *offers her*
*rebuttal.*


ALVITA
Husband Number Four, you *lied.* Tell these
Good people how sometimes nothing could please
You. When the green-eyed monster took over
You weren't yourself. You forgot we were lovers.
You'd rant and rave. You thought poor young Ryan

The student kid – the freckled Scottish one –
With his dark red hair and his tiny bum

RYAN, *who's the kid filming, raises a hand to the audience,
to be acknowledged, but we get no sign that there is anything
between him and* ALVITA.

You'd say I'm eyeing him like I want some
Of that? Please! Not if you died tomorrow!
Meanwhile, you won't even let me *borrow*
The keys to the Subaru! You act like
What is yours is not also mine. You psych
Yourself out, stressing about who owns me,
While you keep your junk under lock and key.
And try to keep me home. But we don't own
Each other. I don't check up on your phone,
Or use GPS to see where you are.
But seems you'd like me locked up in that car!
You *should* be saying:

ALVITA *gets behind* ELRIDGE *and uses him as a ventrilo-
quist's dummy so her voice seems to come out of his mouth while
she controls his movements.*

ALVITA (*AS ELRIDGE*)
                    Alvita, you do you.
Go out and find your joy. I won't do
Anything to block or kill your spirit
Cos I love you and I trust you, innit.

ALVITA
Women like me, we can't love control freaks.
We want to travel, to live, to seek
Fresh pastures, possibilities, new worlds.
We're women. Not children. Not little girls.
The best man of all, blessed and wise, is dead:
Nelson Mandela, cos it's him who said:

*An old man in the Pub Chorus, one of the old regulars we saw
in the opening scene, turns from his pint and takes on the role
of* NELSON MANDELA.

NELSON MANDELA
Resentment is like drinking poison

ALVITA
                                    Yuh see?

39

NELSON MANDELA
And then hoping it will kill your enemies.
And the wisest men know how to rise above
The desire to control the ones you love.

ALVITA
Husbands! Hear these words! Know them to be true.
If you get yours, why d'you care what I do?
Are you lacking something? Are you deprived?
Come sundown, aren't you truly satisfied?

*We see* ALVITA *sidle up to the* AUTHOR *with her mobile.*
*She seems to be asking to jump on the Author's Wi-Fi hotspot,*
*but the* AUTHOR *isn't having it.*

It's like them people who lock up their Wi-Fi . . .
Like, they think it's gonna run out! Like if I
Jump on it, and get something for free,
It's unfair. Not as far as I can see.
Just mind your own business, husbands! Then
I'll mind mine. And peace will reign in Willesden.
But they don't. He's in my face about what
I wear. He's like:

HUSBAND ELRIDGE
                    Please God tell me you're not
Going out in that. The skirt's way too small;
The top's too low; you're barely dressed at all.

ALVITA
And I wait and dare him to speak some more.

HUSBAND ELRIDGE
I'm just saying sometimes you look like a—

ALVITA
STOP RIGHT THERE. Please don't use, my brother,
One type of woman to cuss another.
We are all sisters. And don't try to neg
Me. You feel free to take me down a peg
Or two. Mention my crow's feet. Cellulite.
Tell me I'm boring or not too bright.
Cos you've worked out when I'm shy or sad
I won't stray too far. I won't act too bad.
But when I'm feeling myself; hair done right,
Clothes on point? Then you nuh want me out nights.
When I hit the club, it's full of your spies:
Your cousin, your sister's man. Benny. Mike.
You think your *man dem* can shut *me* down?
Step to me; we'll see who ends 'pon the ground!

And he sees I'm not playing. Then he frets
And feels sorry for himself:

HUSBAND ELRIDGE
                         Don't get
Married. Only two things worse than a wife—

ALVITA
Cue some lame-arse joke about pain and strife . . .
The same sad anti-wife jokes you see online –
What would you'all do without us for punchlines?
You get so dramatic:

HUSBAND WINSTON
                         To love you is hell –
It's like I'm thirsty and you're a dry well.

ALVITA
So *you* say

HUSBAND DARREN
                 It's like being on actual fire –

HUSBAND IAN
Like being thrown on a funeral pyre

HUSBAND ELRIDGE
You're like woodworm

ALVITA
Says *you*

HUSBAND ELRIDGE
     And I'm the tree.
You're not done till you've eaten all of me!

ALVITA
People of Brent: you hear how he talks when
He's pissed? Well, I *told* him he said that then
I used it against him. He never found
Out it wasn't true – I just wrote it down
And said he did. That poor fool got no peace.
I told student Ryan, and Kelly, my niece,

*We see* KELLY, *and see* RYAN *still hidden by his camera
raise a hand, but again in the most casual way.*

And they believed me and blamed *him*; he looked
Like the bad guy and I'm off the hook.
Simple advice, Colin, it'll take you far:
*Whoever's behind the wheel drives the car.*

That's it. We didn't fight, if I'm honest.
He planted his seeds. I burned his forests.

HUSBAND ELRIDGE
I said sorry for things I hadn't done!
Girls I never touched, game I never run.

ALVITA
I knew you too ol' to be playing away
But I accused you of it anyway
Because you liked it! You needed jealousy
To feel I wanted you like you wanted me . . .
I told you: 'All my going out at night
Is just to check those girls I fear might
Be after you!'

HUSBAND ELRIDGE
       And I truly believed.

ALVITA
You were way too vain to think I'd deceived
You. But truth is I'm just out getting mine!
And the thing is, I get my way every time . . .
Women are good at lying! Or if you
Want to say it more nicely, we just do
A little creative work with the facts.

I cry, I make up stuff, I blatantly act –
I'm playing four-dimensional chess,
Colin, and no husband can ever mess
With me. Especially not in a bed.
That's where I truly eff with their heads . . .
For example, if I've got a new man –
A fresh husband; not a flash in the pan –
Lying next to me, and here comes his hand,
I immediately make him understand:
I will get out of this bed unless you
Get me off first. *Then* I'll see what I can do
For you. The point is you don't get someting
For nutting. No my friend: that's not a thing.
And honestly, as it goes, I was not
Attracted to any of those old men. But
I put on a good show. And they gave me
What I was owed, and to speak honestly
I probably stressed them all the time
Because I really hated having to grind
Them at all. But you know what? Even if
The Pope was watching, I'd still call them chiefs,
And fools and eediat. And Christ himself knows:

BLACK JESUS
Even if she went and died tomorrow
No one could say she didn't do her share

Of work in the bedroom. And to be fair
To the husbands, I should mention, Colin,
They did try. To get it up, to put it in . . .
They'd roar like lions, crazy with lust
But every time they tried – it was a bust.

ALVITA *is grateful for* BLACK JESUS's *intervention on
her behalf.*

ALVITA
Then I'd say:

*We see the following acted out between* ALVITA *and*
HUSBAND IAN. ALVITA *starts kind and loving, works
herself up into a comical rage, and then just as abruptly turns
philosophical:*

Oh, babe . . . little man looks small
Tonight. Come here. Kiss me. Don't be all
Down about it. You're always telling me
To take a chill pill. Relax. And just *be.*
So take your own advice. Calm yourself.
Be patient! How come you got all this wealth
But can't get it up? Don't get an attitude!
I'm just saying – I'm not trying to be rude.
Why're you groaning? You wanna get with me?

Mi deh yah\* – I'm right here. Now, you see,
Fact is this pum-pum† could have a good
Time somewhere else – don't mean to kill the mood –
But apparently if I cheat on you
That would make me a 'bad wife' and 'a shrew'.
*Lawd!* The patriarchy! It's like I'm caught
In a trap and it's all your own damn fault!
Oh, we'd have a lot of these little chats . . .
Let's move on. Fourth Husband. We'll get into that:
My fourth husband was a proper player.
We were married but he had a lover.
And I was young, and really feeling myself.

HUSBAND ELRIDGE
Body tight, no one left *her* on the shelf –
Stubborn and wilful; first one on the dance
Floor and last one off.

ALVITA
                                        If I had a chance
To sing I took it. Sweet soul voice I've got
When I'm pissed. When I've had a few shots.

---

\*Patois: 'Everything is good, I'm here, I'm okay.'
†Patois: crude term for 'vagina'.

Me nah braffing.* No, man, I sing like a bird –
Not like these uptight churchy men I've heard
Threaten their wives with hell if they want drink!
If any man thinks he'll stop *me,* best think
Again! Because a Baileys with nuff ice
Gets me in the mood. Makes me feel nice.
And I'm not going to stand here and tell you
That I'm not more likely to want to do
It when I've had a few.

ALL THE WOMEN IN THE PUB
                              Let's all be real.
Sometimes a drink or two helps seal the deal.

ALVITA
Oh, Lawd Almighty! When I think back to
Them days when I was young, I can't do
Nothing but smile. I love to remember
That sweet May time, now I'm in September . . .
I'm still glad I had my time in the sun!
Now I'm old. Boobs hang low. Lost my bum.
But you know what? It's really whatever.

---

*Patois: to boast or take excessive pride in something.

PUBLICAN POLLY
Youth and beauty, they don't last forever.

ASMA
The sweet fruit's gone, there's no juice left behind.

ZAIRE
But I'll still squeeze whatever's left out of the rind!

ASMA
Or, at least, I'll do the best that I can.

ALVITA
But wait up: back to this fourth husband.
To be honest, I got my screwface on
When he chirpsed other women. But I won
In the long run. I didn't cheat but I
Got my flirt on, my come-to-bed eyes . . .

HUSBAND ELRIDGE
Couldn't stand to see her with another man!

ALVITA
Jealousy fried you in your own damn pan!
Oh, I made you a proper hell on earth . . .
This man who bitched like he was in childbirth

If he even stubbed a toe. Not good with pain
That one.

HUSBAND ELRIDGE
And God knows she made me insane
With agony.

ALVITA
          He died not long after
I got back from holiday in Jamaica.
He's buried near here, just by Uncle P
Up Willesden Lane, in that old cemetery.
The headstone's plain as a plate, not my taste –
But paying more for that one'd be a waste,
You get me? Anyway, he's now deceased.
So farewell and God bless him. Rest in peace.
My fifth husband. Okay, here we go. Well,
I actually *don't* hope he rots in hell.
And yet, to be honest, he was the worst.
He'd get physical with me. That's the first
And last time I'll let that happen, I swear.
He hurt me here, there, oh, everywhere . . .
And yet in bed he was so fresh, so fine,
Gave head with such skill, the man took his time,
So even when I was aching from old
Bruises, I could turn his base love to gold.

Can it be I loved him more than the rest
Because he always gave me so much less?
The thing with girls – I'm gonna generalize –
Cos I've noticed it, and I sympathize:

PUBLICAN POLLY
What we can't get easy? That's what we crave.
We get obsessed, we stalk, we don't behave . . .

ZAIRE
Tell us no, we're all over it, we're set:
But come on strong? We lose interest, all bets
Are off. Play hard to get, and we'll chase you,
But act too keen? Then I'm just not that into
You. Masochism, some say, but isn't it
Also just how things work in a market?
Love is capital: this, smart women know.

ALVITA
But I married the fifth one, as it goes,
For love not money – bless him – still a young
Bwoy he was; an Oxford student, just sprung
From college and looking for a flatshare.
He rented a room off my mate Zaire,
My ride-and-die bitch. I tell her everything,
And vice versa. There's no secret I can't bring

Zaire. If my husband pissed up a wall
Or something much worse, it's Zaire I'd call,
Or any girlfriend I know, or my niece,
Kelly . . . He can't make me sign a release
Form! I'll speak! And that's what I kept doing,
Telling his secrets, and he was screwing,
And well-shamed and sorry he ever told
Me any private thing, new or old . . .
But then one day mid-March, it was springtime –
Which is when I like to take some proper 'me time'
At Zaire's; get out of Brent; see some trees
(Cos sistas like the country, too, believe);
And we hung out with this Ryan, Zaire
And me,

ZAIRE

Running round Oxford, here and there;
'Spose we felt we could let our freak flags fly
Hang wid da yute; and, maybe check some guys . . .

ALVITA

But who knew what was in the stars for me?
Where, when and who would be my destiny?
I was just doing my thing: clubbing, nights
Out at student parties; or downing pints
In their weird country pubs, or out raving,

ZAIRE
And always in her tight red dress, leaving
Not a thing to the imagination.
No need to wash it – she always had it on . . .

ALVITA
But let me tell you how it went down:

ALVITA *approaches* RYAN *and starts flirting with him, as she tells her story. Romantic music plays, birdsong: 'Loving youuu . . . is easy cos you're byoootifuuuul . . .'*

Me and this kid, flirting; alone, far from town,
And one day I just say to him, look, man,
If my husband dies, we should make a plan
To marry, okay?

*Sound of record being violently ripped off turntable.* PUB CHORUS *are a bit scandalized to realize Elridge was right about Alvita and Ryan the whole time.* ALVITA *tries to defend herself, like someone on the* Jeremy Kyle Show.

          Cos, people of Brent:
It's about insurance. And in the event
Of . . . *whatever*, I never get married
Without a little something up my sleeve:

Like a good plan B. You don't want to be
That dumb mouse who thinks it's gonna get free
Through the only hole it found in your home –
The same one you just filled with toxic foam . . .
So I told him I loved him like crazy!
My mother taught me that – a smart lady –
I said I dreamt of him regularly,
But in these dreams it seemed like he'd killed me

*This tragic, bloody fantasy is acted out, and then, just as*
*quickly, is revoked.*

Because the bed was totally bloody –
Blood on the sheets, all over my body –
But that's a good sign, cos in the Tarot
Blood's a symbol for gold, far as I know –
But it was all lies! Trust me, I don't waste
Time dreaming of men. That was cut and paste
Out of Mum's playbook. She's my true mentor
When it comes to husbands – and so much more.
But wait – Colin – I've gone and lost my thread –
What was I saying? Right – fourth husband: dead.
And when I saw him laid out at James Crook

*The pub turns into a funeral parlour.*

I got my weep on, and really did look
Gutted, like a proper sad widow should,
And wore a veil. But since I was all good
For husbands, with one lined up round the bend,
I didn't really cry that much, in the end.

ZAIRE
The church service was St Mary's, next day.
Full of local mourners from down our way,
And student Ryan was there in the crowd

ALVITA
And God help me, but I was like *wow*
He's fit, you know! Nice body, tight round bum . . .
He was twenty. I could have been his mum.
Yeah, I was forty, to tell you the truth,
But he's a honey, and I've a sweet tooth –
Plus I'm gap-toothed like Madonna; which suits
Us both; symbolizes passion; it's cute,
It's sexy, and Christ Almighty, I *liked* sex,
I was hot, young-ish, horny, full of next-
Level energy, and had – so husbands
Told me – the best punani in the land!
I'm one of these Venus-born girls for real,
But I've also got this Mars side? I feel
Like Venus gave me my lust and passion,

But Mars made me a woman of action.
Basically I'm Venus with Mars rising,
Which is why I don't get this 'slut-shaming'?
It's sad: I'm just doing me, naturally:
I follow my stars, and they have made me
Unable to ever say a hard no
To a nice, fit bloke who's good to go.
And plus, here's the mark of Mars on my face
(I've got another in a private place)
Which means even though Auntie prays for me,
It does no good. I can't choose carefully.
I'm all instinct. It's whatever feels right.
He can be tall or short or black or white –
I'm not bothered, as long as he feels me.
Don't have to be rich, or have a degree . . .
What can I say?

ZAIRE
                    Something like a month passed
And Al and Ryan got hitched. It was vast,

*The pub turns into a wedding.*

That wedding, they did it in proper style,
And then she signed over to him the pile

Of money, two flats, and the Subaru
That she'd got from leaving the previous two.

ALVITA
Truth be told, I lived to regret that choice.
Ryan, turns out, was a dick. Raised his voice
At me over every likkle ting, left
Me no freedom. See this ear? I'm now deaf
In it, cos he smacked me in my head
For tearing a page from a book he'd just read.

ZAIRE
But he couldn't keep her down. Al's a lion.
Stubborn. And not scared of chiefs called Ryan.
She still cussed him day and night and flexed where
She felt like flexing. Traipsing here and there,
Going round the old flats, which he *hated* –

ALVITA
And he'd start giving off to me, slated
Me, giving it all this 'bout his mate, Mo,
Who spotted his wife in the street with no
Veil on and left her like that!

*We see* RYAN *bringing* ASMA *to tell her story, like an example in an argument.* ALVITA *is unimpressed, as is* ASMA *for being thus used.*

ASMA

                    High and dry,
Haven't seen him since two thousand and five.
Good riddance!

HUSBAND RYAN

                    But what about Ibrahim's
Wife? Went Olympics without asking him.

ASMA

Two thousand twelve. He left. And she's okay!

ALVITA

He'd even dig up the Bible. He'd say:

HUSBAND RYAN

Actually, in Ecclesiastes, there's
Some really quite sensible stuff. Like where
It says: 'Thou shall not let thy wife wander
About.'

ALVITA

  I saw he was getting fonder
Of his own voice. Liked to make pronouncements:

HUSBAND RYAN

If I let my wife wander around Brent
On Halloween, dressed like a 'slutty witch',
What does that make me? Basically, her bitch.
That's like building your house on shifting sand;
That's like trying to catch water in your hand;
That's a bloody mug's game, and I'm no mug!

ALVITA

And on and on. And I was just like: ugh.
I didn't listen to a word of it.
Him nagging, his guilt trips, none of it.
I wasn't going to be preached at by him –
I hate anyone tries to rein me in.
Am I alone, ladies? Didn't think so.
If he could have, he'd've killed me, I know,
But by that point, the feeling was mutual.
So, here's the context I need to give you all.
The real reason I tore that page out his book,
And he box mi left ear wid a right hook:
See, he quoted from this book night and day
It was his Bible.

HUSBAND RYAN
                    My gospels, I'd say,
Of Saints Farrell, Moxon, Peterson, Strauss —

ALVITA
(Like this was a joke to bring down the house.)

HUSBAND RYAN
It's made of some books I've put together,
*Twelve Rules of Life*; *The Myth of Male Power*;
*The Game*; something called *The Woman Racket*;

ALVITA
(Some mental crap he got off the Internet . . . )

HUSBAND RYAN
So then this became my new daily thing:
Whenever I wasn't busy studying
For my Master's —

ALVITA
                    — he read this stuff on crap wives.
He knew more about evil women's lives
Than there are saints in the Good News Bible . . . !
Trust me: your average young man is liable
To believe the only true good woman

In this world is his mum or blessed nan!
The rest of us? Witches, out to get him.


ZAIRE
But who wrote all these books about women?
Mate, if women wrote the books he studied
The list of wives abused, misused, bloodied
Would be longer than the Good Book itself!
It'd be too bloody big to fit on the shelf!


ALVITA
What it is, is: Ryan's under the star
Of Mercury. I'm Venus. So we are
Fundamentally incompatible.
Mercury's maths, it's science: rational.
Venus: she loves to party, spend – and dance.
We're so different we never had a chance.
When one of our stars is high in the sky,
The other must fall. That's the reason why
Young sons of Mercury, like my Ryan,
Get all woman-hating and then buy in
To the claim *we're* the problematic ones!
Then, when they're old, and their hard-ons are gone,
These same professors go and write their tomes
On how we should know our place and stay home!
But to get to the point: I'm telling you

How I got smacked for a book. It's all true:
One night Ryan, this Scottish husband of mine,
Was into his book and reading out lines
About wicked women, starting with Eve,
No less, who wrecked the world, Ryan believed:

HUSBAND RYAN
Cos she's to blame for original sin,
And that's why Christ had to be brought in,
And then killed, so we could be forgiven.

ALVITA
Sure: all the fault of one stupid woman!
Then he's on to how:

HUSBAND RYAN
                        Samson lost his hair:
While kipping. His girl sliced it with a pair
Of shears.

ALVITA
Which somehow made him lose his eyes?
But we're not done: next it's ancient Greek guys.

*Tearing curtains off the windows to use as togas, the* PUB
CHORUS *act out the following scenes:*

He's reading – out loud –

HUSBAND RYAN
                        about Deianira
Who set her man Hercules on fire.
Then it's poor Socrates, whose wife poured piss
On his head. Xanthippe.

ALVITA
                        And the weird thing is
The dyam fool just sit there, like a dead man,
And wipe his forehead, and then all he can
Say is:

SOCRATES
After the thunder, comes the rain.

ALVITA
He'd two wives, that fool, and they both caused him pain.
But the story Ryan most liked to repeat
Was really *nasty*. So, the Queen of Crete –
Pasiphaë – for some reason shagged this bull?
And she gave birth to . . . well, like, not a full
Bull, it was a minotaur? Like, half man –
You know what? No. I can't even stand
To say. Then there's this Clytemnestra bitch

63

Who did the dirty on her man, a sitch
Which led to him dying. Ryan *loved* that.
There was Eriphyle, this girl who, for a fat
Gold chain, sold out her husband, Amphiaraus.
The Greeks demanded to know where he was:

CHORUS OF GREEKS
We suspect he hides somewhere in Thebes!
But where?

ALVITA
And wifey like:

ERIPHYLE
Here. Gold chain, please!

ALVITA
Then on to Livia and Lucilla.
Both of them were stone-cold husband killers.
Liv straight up poisoned hers cos she'd always
Truly hated and dreaded him from day
One. Meanwhile Lucilla's dark devotion
Was so strong she gave her man a love potion
So that he wouldn't chirps no other girls,
But it was toxic – so he left this world.
Point being:

HUSBAND RYAN
                I've read around and I've found
You really can't win if you're a husband.

ALVITA
Then he told me how this Latumius
Was

HUSBAND RYAN
                — bitching to a friend called Arrius
How three of his wives had hung themselves right
In his garden, on a tree, out of spite.

ALVITA
And Arrius is like:

ARRIUS
                Well, listen, mate:
A cutting from that tree would be great,
And I'll plant it in my yard happily!

ALVITA
But it wasn't just old tales he told me.
He read all the latest tabloid nightmares
About husband murderers:

ASMA

                              Who kept their
Husbands' corpses in a cupboard while they
Got hot and heavy with their brand-new bey
In the same room.

ALVITA

                    These stories were hardcore:

*The* PUB CHORUS *ladies read these headlines from trashy*
*supermarket tabloids and magazines.*

ZAIRE
Some had put nails through their brains while they snored
And killed them that way.

PUBLICAN POLLY

                         Some had spiked their drinks.

ALVITA
He'd heard them all. I couldn't bear to think
How many. Plus he knew more anti-wife
Online memes than there are seconds in this life.

*We see these memes projected as huge screenshots on the back*
*wall, texted from Ryan to Alvita.* ZAIRE *reads the captions*
*out loud and takes us through this presentation.*


ZAIRE
'*Happy wife, happy life.* But nothing rhymes
With *Happy Husband*, ever wonder why?
*Welcome to married life, dumbass.*' That's one.
There's the one with the guy who looks done,
Sitting on the street, tragic-looking fella –
'Saw his face and offered him a dollar:
He said: *I'm not homeless, I'm married!*'
Like a wife is a terminal disease.
Or on a napping Kim K it'll say:
*Sleeping Beauty: cute by night, whore by day.*


ALVITA
Can you imagine how much it hurt me
To listen to this pure misogyny?
And when I saw him about to restart
Reading that damn book:

*We see this vital re-enactment:*

ZAIRE

                    She tore it apart,
Tore three pages while he was reading them:

ALVITA

And I'm not the strongest, but there and then
I pulled back my fist and clocked him proper
Hard on his cheek. He fell. Came a cropper
In the fireplace, arse over tit. Then rose
Up, raging like a pitbull, then *he* chose
To get up and strike *me* upside my head.
I hit the floor, and lie down like mi dead.

ZAIRE

And when he saw how very still she lay,
He was bricking it. Almost ran away,
But then she come to and raised up her head.

ALVITA

*Rare*, you for real tried to kill me!

ZAIRE

                    She said.

ALVITA
You'd kill me for the cash, the Subaru,
This flat? Well, 'fore I die, let me kiss you!

ZAIRE
And he came to her side and knelt right down,
Full of shame and with his heart in his mouth,
He said:

HUSBAND RYAN
       I love you, darling Alvita,
I swear to God I will never beat yer.
Though it was sort of your fault that I did,
I hope you'll find it in your heart to forgive.

ALVITA
So I punched him again, hard with my fist,
And said: 'Listen, teef! Too late, you've missed
Your chance. I'm dying. And done talking to you.'
But as it goes, and after we'd talked it through
A long time, we did manage to agree . . .
That everything would be decided by me:
The flat stayed in my name, and the motor,
Boy can't move without checking my rota.
And now that I run tings completely
You'll hear him say:

HUSBAND RYAN

               Oh, my amazing wife,
Do whatever you want with your own life;
What's best for you is clearly best for me.

ALVITA
And after that day, we had no more beef.
Lawd, for a kinder wife you couldn't arks
If you searched from India to Denmark.
And to be fair, he's also kind to me.
I pray to God – well, through my Auntie P –
To bless him, seeing as now he submits
To me. Right: my tale. You still up for it?

*There is encouraging applause from the* PUB AUDIENCE,
*but as it dies down, we hear one loud, somewhat contemptuous
laugh rise above the rest, until it is the only voice left. Everyone,
including* ALVITA, *looks for the source, and finds it is smug*
PASTOR JEGEDE. ALVITA *is unamused.*

ALVITA
Excuse me: did I say something funny?

PASTOR JEGEDE
Oh, sister, I think that was easily
The longest introduction I have heard,
It seemed to be at least eight thousand words!

PASTOR JEGEDE *keeps on laughing and* ALVITA *looks like she's about to go for him, but she's held back by* BARTOSZ, *a beefy-looking Polish man, who steps forward to confront the* PASTOR.

ALVITA (*ASIDE, TO THE AUDIENCE*)
Bartosz. A bailiff. Does what needs doing.

BARTOSZ
I can't believe, for me is amusing:
Why men of church always put nose in
Where don't belong? How I can listen him?
Man of church is like fly. Always he's in,
Everything. Like fly. See he falls in food,
In business, everything! No, is not good.
He says 'long'. But how he is saying long
When he is interrupt? When *he* makes long!
This woman, good woman, she tell story.
Never is boring. No, *he* is boring.

PASTOR JEGEDE
This is your opinion. But I could tell
Some stories about bailiffs and the hell
They put good people through – bailiffs like you –
And we'd laugh, and know who is the buffoon.

BARTOSZ
I am bailiff, yes, but I curse your face!
I am cursing men of church in this place!
Many, many story I can tell from
My country! My story are very strong,
You can say this? Strong? And make shame to you,
And you will not like because story is true!

PUBLICAN POLLY
All right, simmer down: that's enough of that!
Let her get on with . . . what she's getting at.
I'm surprised at you, Father: you two sound
Like two pissheads, brawling. Trust me, around
Here we get enough of that. Alvita?

ALVITA
Always ready to speak verse in meter!
I mean, *if* it's okay with Pastor here . . .

PASTOR JEGEDE
Please, go on with your tale: I am all ears.

# THE WIFE OF WILLESDEN'S TALE

FIRST CHILD *walks across the stage – like a scene changer in a medieval revel – holding an enormous sign which reads:*

## THE WIFE OF WILLESDEN'S TALE

SECOND CHILD *walks in the opposite direction with an equally large sign:*

Transferred from Arthurian Camelot
to Maroon Town, Jamaica

FIRST CHILD *walks by once more with the sign:*

Featuring Queen Nanny!
Famed rebel slave and leader of peoples!

*As before,* ALVITA *tells the story but the* PUB CHORUS *dramatizes it.*

AUNTIE P
Back in the Maroon days of Queen Nanny,
Who Jamaicans love to the $n$th degree

All the island full up ah duppy*,
And all kind ah spirit a roam free . . .
River Mumma hide a golden table
Under her skirts, and Ol' Higue
She suck de breath from de sleeping baby –

ALVITA
At least, that's what my Auntie P told me:
We're talking way back in the seventeen twenties,
Bit before my time. Now'days no one sees
Ghosts or spirits or witches or duppy
Cos the island full up with nuff pastor,
Preachermen, vicar and minister,
Witnesses and Seventh-day Adventists,
Latter-day Saints, Catholics and Baptists,
Who spend their days hunting for evil deeds,
In every field and yard and running stream;
Dash round blessing anyone they can reach,
They're every-damn-where like sand on a beach;
Blessing dance halls, cafes, hotels, high schools,
Nightclubs, hairdresser's, sports grounds, swimming pools.
And why would the spirits wan' deal with that?
Wherever di duppy dem used to be at

---

*A malevolent spirit or ghost. River Mumma and Ol' Higue are both fearsome female figures from Jamaican folklore.

Now preacherman ah go all round
Praying for your soul, kneeling 'pon de ground,
And asking God to have mercy on us.
Jamaican women these days make no fuss
About fearing duppy; they're too busy
Avoiding these churchmen who wan' weigh she
Down with sin. Anyway: our Queen Nanny
Had a young buck Maroon in her army
Who one day rode to Cudjoe's Leeward Land,
Where he saw a beautiful, young Akan
Girl, early one morning, just walking by,

*We see this re-enacted by* DARREN *and* KELLY.

A virgin, with no interest in this guy,
But he wouldn't stop.

*Pause.*

                    He thought his strength gave
Him the right.

*Longer pause.*

            Well, Cudjoe Town was outraged
By this criminal oppression, and so

Many protested to Captain Cudjoe
That the young Maroon was condemned to death,
By the law courts of St Elizabeth.
Now, that was the sentence of judge and jury –
But Queen Nanny and some Windward ladies
Begged the Captain to

THREE WINDWARD LADIES
                Tink again and give
This bad young bwoy to us and let him live,
And leave the Leeward, and give Nanny a shot
At deciding whether to kill him or not.

ALVITA
Nanny was glad the King had changed his tune –
The boy came. And she said to this Maroon:

QUEEN NANNY
Yuh nuh outta trouble yet! Mi might still
Kill you. But capital punishment will
Only go so far. I'm interested in
Restorative justice. Understanding
Who you hurt and why. So here is my deal:
You'll live – *if* you can tell me what *we* feel –
I mean we women. What *we* most desire.
You tell me that? I won't set you on fire.

And if you don't have the answer right now
I give you permission to leave this town
A year and a day. Wherever you go
Ask everybody you meet if *they* know.
But before you leave, you must guarantee
That when 'Time's up' you come straight back to me.

ALVITA
This young Maroon was proper screwing
Because suddenly he wasn't doing
Whatever he wanted. He had no choice
But to submit to the powerful voice
Of Queen Nanny, and start on his journey,
Then come back in a year on bended knee,
To this Queen, with an answer that would fly.
So off he rode, feeling very hard done by.
This bwoy went everywhere, to every yard,
Looking for anyone who had thought hard
About

YOUNG MAROON
        Wat women want and love the most,
From the Blue Mountains to town and coast,
Me can't find no one, enslaved or free,
Fi give me answers wat mek wi all agree!

ALVITA
Some said:

*Here members of the* PUB CHORUS, *as well as some of Alvita's* HUSBANDS, *interject:*

HUSBAND WINSTON
            The thing women love most is money.

ALVITA
Some said:

HUSBAND IAN
            They're drawn to power like bears to honey!

ALVITA
Some said:

AUNTIE P
            Personally, I'm quite fond of jewels . . .

ZAIRE
Women want actual orgasms, you fools!
And to have multiple partners – unjudged.

ALVITA
But some said:


HUSBAND ELRIDGE
    Give me a break. Can we please not fudge
The issue. Admit you're most satisfied
When we worship you with flattering lies!


ALVITA
And you know, if you put the lying part
Aside, it's fair to say we'll give our hearts
To that person who brings us attention,
Takes care of business and, yes, who mentions
The good things about us. But that's just love!
Now, some went proper *deep*. Some said:


*We are surprised to find the women with the deepest thoughts
are people we've hardly noticed up to now:* KELLY, *Alvita's
niece;* PUBLICAN POLLY; *and* ASMA, *the young rebel
wife. They all now stand to speak, and with an intensity that
changes the atmosphere in the pub. They speak in their natural
accents – Black-British Kilburn for* KELLY, *Pakistan-
inflected for* ASMA *– but the words themselves seem to come
from a transnational sacred text of rights and duties. These
women are bearing witness to a truth.*

KELLY

                              Above
All things, we want freedom. Freedom to know
Our own desires. We want to follow
Them where they lead.


ASMA

                    We want to be free from
The bitter critique of men, banging on
And on about our apparent failings.


PUBLICAN POLLY
We want to hear no more of men saying
We have no judgement or reason. We are
Also wise.


ALVITA *breaks the spell of solemnity.*

ALVITA
                Yes, wise enough to know where our
Sore spots are. Where the truth hurts. If you ask
To touch us there, there's a kick up the arse
For telling us the bit we don't want to
Hear or take on board. Come try it and you'll

See. We nuh easy! Not women nor girls.
Still, it's nice to think we're perfect angels . . .
Now, some said:

*We see Colin's fiancée* SOPHIE, *now dressed like an eighteenth-century British woman on the island, fanning herself from the heat.*

SOPHIE
                    What we *so* appreciate
Is being considered, as women, great
And loyal friends. Who can keep a secret,
Choose a purpose, and be steadfast to it.
And who never betray a confidence.

ALVITA
Maybe you think that all makes perfect sense,
But, we have a saying round here: *Finger*
*Neber say: 'Look here,' 'im say: 'Look yonder.'*
Meaning: people don't like to point out their
Own flaws? But I know women tell and share
Secrets. If they say they don't they're lying.
'S'like that tale I read in that book of Ryan's
About King Midas – you wanna hear it?

*The* PUB CHORUS *look at each other and then with slight weariness grab their curtain-togas again for this brief interlude. Throughout the next section,* RYAN *plays King Midas. We may get the sense, as the story progresses, that* ALVITA *is talking less about Midas's dirty secret as much as Ryan's marital failings, principally his domestic abuse, which is a secret, of course, that Alvita has refused to keep . . . And as they tell the apparently frivolous story of Midas, we sense a more serious subtext beneath.*

ALVITA
Won't take a minute: this one's Ovid,
Roman poet. He wrote this likkle ting:
That under Midas's long hair, the King
Had two big ol' donkey ear, which he hid,
Right, because you would. And he truly did
It well. *So* well, that only his own wife
Knew it. And he trusted her with his life.
He begged her:

HUSBAND RYAN
             Tell no one. Never confess
My sad, deforming, secret ugliness.

ALVITA

And she promised she never would. She flat
Out *swore* she would never do him like that.
No, not for the world would she drag his name
Through the streets. Honestly, *she'd* be ashamed.
But then the thing was: it was killing her
To have to keep this secret forever.
She was heart-sick. Like, a physical pain?
What she had to say she couldn't contain
Inside her. And because she didn't dare
Tell no one, she dashed down to this marsh where
Some water was – and, with her heart on fire,
Booming like pub lady at closing hour –
She put her mouth to the water and cried:
'*Water, keep my secret! What I say hide*
*Deep within you. But between you and me?*
*My man him have long ears just like donkey!*
*Now that's better. I feel calm and at peace.*
*Couldn't keep that secret no longer, believe.*'

*At some point during this retelling,* RYAN *raises a hand to*
*hit* ALVITA *again, but she catches it by the wrist, and holds*
*it up as a shameful object for the audience to see.*

ALVITA
That's it. We can lie and push it all down
Till we just can't. Time's up. Truth gets around.

*The melancholy tone suddenly switches, and ALVITA's back
to her playful self.*

For more Midas – if that's your cup of tea –
Go to O, Ovid: Kilburn Library.
Back to this Maroon I was discussing:
When he understood it was not nuffing
To find out what women them love the best
Him heart sunk low in him sorrowful chest.
But it was time: he could put it off no
Longer. He had to face Nanny and go
Home. And on the way back, so sad and stressed,
He found himself in a green wilderness,
Where he saw a whole heap of young gal dem
Dancing on the forest floor, in tandem . . .

*We see this dance, as some of the young women of the* PUB
CHORUS *get up and do a routine: the Cameo Slide Dance.*
ALVITA *joins them. The scene is lit so as to suggest these girls
might be spirits or apparitions of some kind . . .*

And he started walking towards the dance
Thinking

YOUNG MAROON
I'll ask *these* girls: this is my chance!

ALVITA
But 'fore fi him leg reach, them up and fly.
Completely vanished! Who knows how or why . . .
There wasn't a soul left in that forest
'Cept, on the grass sat an old wife. Honest,
You never see such a muss-muss woman
In your life. Ugly. And she raise her hand
And say:

*We see* AUNTIE P *dressed up to resemble a foul, troll-like old Obeah woman.*

OLD WIFE
Young bwoy! You c'yannot pass troo here.
But tell me what you seek; speak in my ear,
Maybe it turn out I can help you, man!
Dere's tings only ol' women unnerstan'.

YOUNG MAROON
Oh, Auntie, I'm really struggling, you know?
Truth is, I'm a dead man if I can't show
I know what women want most on this earth.
If you know, I'll pay you . . . whatever works.

OLD WIFE
If *you* will swear that the next ting I ask
You to do, *you will do*. You can't pass,
Or say no. And if these terms be all right
I'll give you your answer before tonight.

YOUNG MAROON
Yes, Auntie. I'll do whatever it is.

OLD WIFE
Then all will be good, young man, I promise.
Your life is safe; I am your guarantee
And I've no doubt Queen Nanny will agree.
Would that lofty woman – who runs tings here,
In her tall headcloth, with her shining spear –
*Dare* to say no to what *I* come to teach?
But no more talking: let's go so we reach . . .

ALVITA
Then she whispered something in his ear,
She tol' him:

OLD WIFE
       Be happy; be free of fear . . .

*The pub transforms into Queen Nanny's stronghold.*

ALVITA
When they reached Nanny's stronghold, this Maroon
Said:

YOUNG MAROON
   Promise kept – down to the afternoon!
And I'm ready with my answer for you.

ALVITA
Every woman in Windward had come to
Hear: wives, young servant girls, plenty widow –
All of them wise – and Queen Nanny, yuh know,
Sitting in her throne, eager like the rest.
She chose the hour: the boy came for his test.

QUEEN NANNY
I want silence from each and every one
Of you. I want to hear this young boy run
His mouth.

ALVITA
                    And him nah speak quiet like mouse:
Him open his mouth and bring down de house!

YOUNG MAROON
Queen Nanny, who rules this place with iron fist:
The thing women want is basically this:
They want their husbands to consent, freely;
To *submit to their wives' wills* – which should be
Natural in love; for we submit to love.

*Pause.*

To keep power, and have no man above
Them – all women want this. And you can kill
Me, but I speak the truth. Do what you will.

ALVITA
And no wife or widow in Nanny Town
Could disagree with how he broke it down.

They all felt he deserved to keep his life.
But soon as she hear, up stands the old wife:

OLD WIFE
Wait now: I found this boy 'pon de grass.
Lawd-a-mercy, Queen Nanny! 'Fore you pass
Out of dis place, I truly, humbly arks
You to do right by me. That is your task.
*I* gave this answer to the boy. And he
Made a very solemn promise to me:
That if he lived, he'd do what I asked him
To do, no matter what it was. Now, in
Sight of all Windward people: on my life,
Maroon boy, you swore I'd become your wife.
You know *dyam well* I saved your brown backside.
And if I'm lying, tell me how and why.

*Now when* YOUNG MAROON *speaks, he sounds less like
an eighteenth-century soldier, and more and more like a young
man from The Ends.*

YOUNG MAROON
Oh, mate . . . How is this even happening?
Have you seen yourself? Look, I'm promising
I'll give you something else. Choose anything.
You can take all my creps, my diamond rings,

But please leave my body! *It's my body.*

OLD WIFE
Say this, and a curse falls on you and me!
I may be too old and ugly and poor
But there's nothing in this life I want more
Than to be your wife. Won't swap it for all
The jewels in your ear or creps in your hall.
I mean to be your wife, and even above
That, I mean to be, Maroon boy, your love!

YOUNG MAROON
Your what now? Er, you can't be serious?
I am a Maroon. We're imperious
People: we control our own destinies.
I can't marry a . . . *hag.* Nah, that ain't me.

ALVITA
So *he* said. But it made no difference.
He had to marry her – he'd no defence –
He took his old, poor, muss-muss wife to bed.
Now, some theatre-critic types will say
That I'm lazy and should add to the play
A scene from the wedding. With all the joy
And beautiful outfits the hag and boy
Wore, and the feast, and all that. Let's be clear:

There weren't no joy. Only sadness and fear.
He wed her in total secret, next day.
And all day after that he hid away
Like a mole, from his poor, old muss-muss wife,
Desperate and sad at the state of his life.
He was so cut up about it when he
At last came to bed, he thrashed in the sheets,
While his wife lay there watching all the while.
And she said – while wearing a great big smile –

OLD WIFE
Oh, my likkle husband, blessings to you!
Do all Maroons treat their wives like you do?
Can this be the law in Queen Nanny's land?
Does each Maroon wife have an awful man?
Young'un, I'm your love. I'm also your wife.
I am she that come fi save yer dyam life!
You and I know that I've done right by you.
So how you ah go treat me like me foofool?
Yuh a gwaan like seh yu head nuh good.
Please tell me what I did to you? You should
Explain – Lawd knows – so I can fix it up.

YOUNG MAROON
Listen: you think you didn't stitch me up?
Look at my situation! Tell me how
Any of this can be 'fixed up'? Come on, now.
You're so butters* and old – and honestly?
You're from trash . . . Yeah, you're too ghetto for me!
You think it's weird that I'm thrashing in bed?
Wish my heart would buss up and leave me dead!

OLD WIFE
And that's the only reason you're upset?

YOUNG MAROON
Oh, my days, woman – don't you get it yet?

OLD WIFE
Well, Maroon boy, I could fix all a dat
If I so chose, in about tree days flat,
*If* you just treat me a likkle bit kind.
But your ideas about good men I find
Ignorant. You think because you born high,
And your family have money, by and by,
That will make you a noble or good man?

---

*Old Weezian term meaning 'unattractive'.

For arrogance like that I got less than
No respect. The proper good man always
Is him who sets himself a goal each day
To do as many good deeds as he can –
That's what I will call a real gentleman.
It's from the likes of Christ we learn kindness,
Not from aristocrats and dey riches.
Cos even if you descended from them
And you got the same high-born fancy name,
You will still inherit nutting at all –
No one does. Just cos your pa act moral
Or your grampa, it don't pass down to you!
No matter how much dey wished that it do.
Some people quote de poets but I like
The wisdom of the yard and the street life,
And there you hear the simple people say:
*Ebry day fishing day, but ebry day*
*No fe catch fish.** And God mean it that way.
Not all of de men can be good all day.
It's *hard* to be good. And from our elders
We catch nutting but our bodies. Shelter
For a while, till dem frail, and die . . . Yes, sir!
Goodness ain't passed down like your hair colour
Maroon boy, everybody knows the truth.

---

*Patois: 'Reward does not always follow labour.'

If all it took to be noble was roots
In some old family plot, then these clans
From H'england – with dey grand old posh names and

*It might be fun to have a family tree projected somewhere on the
back wall, or to have this imagined family otherwise drama-
tized on stage.*

Sugar wealth – they'd shine, all generations.
But *he* beat his wife. *He* ran plantation.

*Pause, as everyone on stage starts to recognize the wisdom of
the* OLD WIFE, *and gather round her, as round a fire, which
fire we now see.*

Imagine I get a burning bush, and I take
It to the darkest house 'tween here and Lake
Victoria. And I just shut the door
And come home. Ya nah see it burn no more
Or less than if twenty thousand men see
It burn? Fire don't need witness to be
Fire. It burn naturally then it go
Out. Will looking at it change it? Lawd, no.
So do you see how goodness in a man
Got nutting to do with who's in his clan?

People act like dey gonna act, like fire.
Can't make dem do as you yourself desire.
No matter the posh names they've been given,
Sons of high-born often turn out villain.

*Now, as* ALVITA *speaks, we see the* OLD WIFE, *agreeing
and supporting her, thankful for her intervention.* ALVITA
*speaks to the real theatre audience, and perhaps comes out to
walk amongst them.*

ALVITA
There's probably a few of you who are feeling
Yourselves, because you're old money, reeling
It in; and you're called Rees-Mogg or what have
You: Don't you know you can still be a chav
In your soul? What have you done? Not a thing.
Depend on your family for everything.
Maybe your grandad was someone. Maybe
Your mum. What have you actually achieved?
Nowt. An old name doesn't make you classy,
That won't cut it, nor your daddy's money,
Real class is a gift from God. It's pure grace.
It don't come from Eton or that other place.
Think about how noble Marley himself
Was. Him rise from poverty to great wealth,

But it was his ideas that made him kind
And good: *None but ourselves can free our minds.**

OLD WIFE
Dear husband, I must say it seems to me –
Even though my people are poor, country
Folk – I might be able to live a good
Life, God-willing, and do the things I should.
I'll call myself good only when I start
Switching sinfulness for good in my heart.
And when you cuss me for being so poor –
Who wore just sandals and asked for no more?
In radical poverty he lived life
And surely any man, young gal, or wife
Will understand what was good enough
For a poor Nazareth boy is sure nuff
Good enough for me. No shame in being
Poor. Or satisfied with enough. Seeing
Them fools who wan be rich above all things –
But never can be? Those men *suffering*.
But the man who say *enough* is content,
Even if he has no shirt. That man want
Nothing. He is wealthy in his own soul.
Even if you call him a criminal.

---

*Marley actually borrowed this line from Marcus Garvey.

ALVITA

> True poverty sings, in reality!

*At this point a small circle of* GOSPEL SINGERS, *who sit at the table with* PASTOR JEGEDE, *stand up and begin singing the refrain 'True poverty sings, in reality' in a Gospel style. At first it seems beautiful – a renouncing of the logic of capital, in which a person's worth is determined by their wealth. But, as* PASTOR JEGEDE *– who we might notice looks conspicuously wealthy, with many gold rings and chains – stands on a table to give his smug homily, and* CHURCH USHERS *move around the Colin Campbell with plates, collecting money from variously willing people,* ALVITA *– and the audience – begins to suspect that the radical vision of Christ is being transformed into something else entirely.* ALVITA, *we notice, refuses point blank to put money on the plate, and the next thing she says is said with a certain irony:*

ALVITA

And Pastor speaks of it *so* pos'tively:

PASTOR JEGEDE

One great blessing of poverty is when
A thief comes near a poor man, well, then,
That poor man has no reason to worry.
No thief comes to *his* door! He'll be merry!

Yes, in some ways it's awful, poverty.
But it's motivating! Keeps you busy.
It can be very educational
Especially if you are rational
And patient in accepting it. It may
Seem miserable. But at least you can say:
'Poverty's mine: you can't take it from me!
I'm perfectly poor, and poor perfectly!'
And often poverty brings you so low
It actually brings you to God! Also,
You'll find out a lot about the real you.
It's like a mirror – I find this so true –
In which you find out who your real friends are.

*The collection finished*, PASTOR JEGEDE *steps down from his pulpit. He notices the* OLD WIFE *waiting for a blessing, and gives her a cursory one – though he seems more interested in the plate that is being returned to him and which he now smoothly empties into his pockets, before sitting back down, satisfied. The* OLD WIFE *looks unsure of his sermon – and the sincerity of his blessing – but shrugs and decides to use its dubious message for her own purposes.*

OLD WIFE
As you've heard, I've done nothing to you, sir!
Even if I'm poor, I won't let you scold

Me for it. Now, you blame me cos I'm old.
I can't find where it says it in the books,
But I know polite people say when you look
'Pon an ol' man, try to be kind with him.
Say: 'sir' or 'uncle' – show respect to him.
And them who write books say the same, I guess . . .
You say I'm old and ugly. But confess
That means you don't need to worry I cheat.
Cos being poor and ugly is a sweet
Way to keep a person faithful always
Until the bitter end of both of your days.
But I've seen: you're basic. You've had your say:
For *you* looks matter. Okay. Have your way.
But choose now. Which one of these will you try:
To have me old and ugly till I die
And be a dedicated, loving wife
Who will please you all the days of your life?
Or you can have me younger and pretty
But take the risk, when we're up in the city,
That every handsome young bwoy wan kiss me,
Here, there, and places you c'yant even see!
The choice is yours: you must do as you feel.

ALVITA
And the boy thought deeply: he stressed and sighed,
Then he turned to his old wife and replied:

YOUNG MAROON
You know what? You're my girl, my wife, my love,
You blatantly know a lot about stuff.
I'll put myself in your hands – you decide.
Choose the best thing, or what makes you feel pride
In both of us. I'm easy. You do you.
If you're into it, I'm, like, on board, too . . .

*We see the* OLD WIFE *tying a silk scarf around his eyes, a blindfold, which seems like it might be borrowed from someone's boudoir. She ties his hands behind his back with another silk scarf. And then changes places with* ALVITA, *who takes it from here, while the* YOUNG MAROON *becomes more obviously* DARREN. *We hear Chaka Khan's 'I'm Every Woman' playing. The next scene between* ALVITA *and* DARREN *feels very intimate, like an erotic scene from their real life.*

ALVITA
So now you agree: I am the master?
I'm in control? Not *ask him* but *ask her*?

HUSBAND DARREN
Yes, my wife, I know now that you know best.

ALVITA
Kiss me, bwoy . . . No more fighting, no more stress.
I swear I'll be every woman to you:
Fit and good and smart and true.
I swear to God I'd rather die crazy
Than be anything but the best lady
Wife this world ever saw. I'll be so good
To you, baby. And in a sec you should
See before you the fittest, finest Fly
Gal you ever seen. Beyoncé look dry
Next to me. Jourdan Dunn an old skinny
Bird next to me. I outshine Naomi.
And if you discover I tell a lie
My life is yours: I'm not afraid to die.
Now let me take this off so you can see
This make-over that has come over me!

ALVITA *pulls off the blindfold to reveal her fabulous, thick,*
*middle-aged beauteousness. And* DARREN *looks delighted,*
*though some of* ALVITA*'s descriptions of what happens next*
*seem almost like magical commands that impel him to act as*
*she says he did.*

ALVITA

Yes, man. When the young boy saw all of *this*,
How young she was and how totally fit,
He hug her up tight-tight in his big arms.
His heart was so uplifted by her charms.
He was all over her . . . simply obsessed . . .

ALVITA *pauses in her narrative for a gratuitous kiss of panto-
mime length.*

He submitted – and she was his the rest
Of the time. Did the sorts of things he liked
And brought nothing but pleasure to their life.
And that's how they spent their lives together.
Hashtag *blessed*. Oh, Lawd Jesus Christ, forever
Send us meek, young husbands who are good in bed
And let us long outlive the men we wed!
And as for those wastemen who won't be ruled
By their wives, I pray the Lord makes those fools'
Lives short. All those old, angry, stingy men.
May you be cussed down high road and back again!

*The* CROWD *in the Colin Campbell give a great cheer – and
hopefully the real audience, too.*

*The stereo comes back on, the pub reverts to a normal night, everybody talking, laughing, drinking.* ALVITA *is dancing with all her* HUSBANDS, *dead and alive . . . The scene seems about to fade out, but the* AUTHOR *makes her way through the crowd to give her retraction.*

# A RETRACTION

AUTHOR

So, yeah . . . No more couplets . . . That shit's *exhausting* to write . . . No, I'm just taking my leave of you . . . Chaucer called this bit the Retraction . . . and I just want to say I hope you had a good time, but if you didn't, listen: blame me . . . And all credit to Chaucer if you liked it – he's the source of all the actual wisdom . . . But, look, on the other hand, if it annoyed or offended you in some way, that's just a lack of finesse on my part, probably . . . so don't blame Chaucer . . . I take full responsibility . . . and while I'm here, back in The Ends, I might as well offer a broader sort of apologia to Brent, as a whole? So: sorry for all the swearing and cultural appropriation in my first book . . .

*As this retraction is made, we see different bits of the apology directed at different characters – all of whom are busy dancing or drinking or celebrating – and who either pay no notice or take the apologies directed at them in a variety of ways. The swearing apology is directed at Alvita's religious relatives – though* AUNTIE P *is entirely unmoved by it – while* ZAIRE

109

*basically accepts the sex apology.* ASMA *and* BARTOSZ *hear her out on the cultural appropriation, although with some scepticism, and so on . . .*

And a bit more cultural appropriation and heresy in the second . . . and the dodgy sex in the third; um . . . the existential bleakness of the fourth . . . er . . . I could go on—

ALVITA
Hush up! Dance!

AUTHOR
Basically, forgive me, Brent! Have mercy on me!

*The* AUTHOR *joins* ALVITA *in a how-low-can-you-go dance-off as the lights fade, and the scene ends . . .*

## About the Author

Zadie Smith is a novelist and essayist. She is the author of seven volumes of fiction and three essay collections. Since 2010 she has been a professor of creative writing at New York University. She is a member of both the American Academy of Letters and the Royal Society of Literature. *The Wife of Willesden* is her first work for the stage.

# Acknowledgements

Thank you to Yvonne Bailey-Smith, Ben Bailey-Smith, Luke Smith, Nick Laird and Indhu Rubasingham for the early reads and edits.

Thank you to Carolyn Cooper CD, Professor of Literary and Cultural Studies at the University of the West Indies, Mona, Jamaica, for her edits, insight and time.